I0555317

Cooking with God

A Grinder – So must we be all ground as fine wheat

Isaiah 28:28

It is through the fire that we are tested so we can stand strong in the face of adversity.

1 Corinthians 3:13

By

Kathy Lee

Cooking With God!

A Gift To:

From:
Date:

Dedication:

To my grandmother (deceased) from whom I got the love for cooking.
This book is dedicated to you.

To my sisters: Marclyn & Karen where we share so many recipes and menus.
Geselle who inspires us with healthy versions of food.
To Donna, whose influence of the various spices and flavors of the many cultures, inspired the dream of one day opening such a place where food, men and women can get together and fellowship.

You are in my thoughts as I write.

Then God said, "I will give you every seed-bearing plant on the face of the whole earth and every tree that has fruit with seed in it. They will be yours for food".

CONTENTS

CONTENTS

Foreword

It takes a great deal more than cooking well to be a great chef, as you will see in the following pages.
Just as it takes a great deal of attributes to be a great man or woman of God.

The Attributes you need to be a chef are, at most, the same attributes it takes to be a man or woman of God, following Him and serving Him in spirit and in truth.

A quality chef can inspire a restaurant's loyalty, just as a man or woman of God can inspire people to be followers of Christ.
All we need are the right measurements and ingredients of Prayer, Fasting, Worship, Waiting, Faith, Wisdom, Trust, and Understanding of God and His word.
When the portions of problems are too much, check the weight of our ingredients for Faith, Prayer, Fasting, Waiting, Worship, and Obedience.

Cooking with God

Introduction

This book is inspired because God sees my passion for cooking.
I find immense joy in cooking.
Whilst I am cooking, I worship, I dance, and I just talk to God. He keeps me company.
My happy place is in the kitchen preparing food.

I love calling neighbors, family, and friends to partake of these meals.
Have you ever been to someone's home, and everyone is always gathered in the kitchen?
There is always light banter while food is being cooked, and the kitchen is always a place of comfort. It's an active hub of chatter, laughter, as well as tears.
You share dreams, comfort each other, have heart-to-heart talks, hugs, tears, good and bad news over coffee and tea…. Sometimes a snack or a plate of food is included.
People say if the walls could talk, I say if the kitchen could talk!

It was while cleaning chicken one day that the Lord asked me, "When are you going to start this book?"
I asked: "What book, Lord?" very confused.
His response: "Cooking with Me"
I just finished my first book (Challenges of Life and the Fruit of the Holy Spirit) and have not even published it yet, as I did not have the financial capacity to do so.
But He makes provision for the vision.

Food is particularly important to the Lord, as we see at the start in Genesis that He provided for Adam and Eve.
We see that He provided daily manna to the Israelites on their journey from Egypt to the Promised Land.
In 1 Kings 17:2-6, God ordered the ravens to feed Elijah, and in verses **15-16**, we see how the widow woman fed Elijah as God commanded her.

God gives us daily manna, whether it be Spiritual food or physical food. He feeds us daily.

Cooking with God

Introduction

What I also know is that the Lord hates waste, and we see evidence of this in the gospel of **John 6:12**. He asked the disciples to gather up what was left so that nothing is lost. They gathered 12 baskets of leftovers!

A good thing would be to feed the hungry, so that nothing is thrown away.

If you must throw it away, please repent for wasting.

Have you ever noticed that mothers put less food for themselves when feeding the family, as they eat what is left on the plates? At least I did that. I hate to waste!

This book is written to give a spiritual side as well as the physical attributes of cooking and all that goes into cooking, and how we, as a chef and a Chef of God, contribute.

Introduction

Master Chef Jesus is in the Kitchen, and I am just the sou chef following His directions.

He will be using **His basic Ingredients** in His menus:

His Word (Prayer)   *Anointing Oil*
Worship   *Trust*
Faith   *Fasting*

Cooking Times: Consistent Prayer. Remember a chef must perfectly time his food. With God, His time is not our time. ***Psalm 31:15*** – Our times are in His hands.

Temperatures: two basic temperatures needed:
    Fire of The Holy Spirit
    Fire of Shadrach; Meshach, and Abednego

Temperatures *may vary based on the season of your life. Which can also be of a cold temperature.*
Cold temperatures *can mean you are not in the place that God wants you, or cold can be used to help mold and bring you together with Him*

All recipes have ingredients and instructions.
Just as the Lord operates. He gives us the ingredients (Word, Prayer, Fasting, Worship, and Faith), and the answers are wrapped in His instructions (Obedience, Trust, and Wait).

His measurements are in cups. What represents 1 cup to us, with the Lord, His cup runneth over (***Psalm 23:5***)
1 Corinthians 10:16 – The cup of blessing that we bless, is it not a participation of the Blood of Christ? The bread that we break, is it not the participation in the body of Christ?

The format of this book will be the physical side of a recipe and a spiritual recipe.
It is aligned with the 15 must-have qualities that make a great chef. (From Forketers)
The meanings of the qualities are given and developed into physical and spiritual attributes and recipes.

The Kitchen

The kitchen is a place where food is prepared, kept, and cooked. (Oxford Dictionary).
Biblically, the kitchen represents our hearts! A place of preparation, to be used by God.
The two main areas in the kitchen are the Stove and the Pantry. They have their own chapters.
There are also kitchen utensils and methods of cooking.

The kitchen is where we all gather. It's a place of sharing not only food but stories of pain, and of joy. It's a place of celebration, a place of comfort, and more importantly, a place where there is unity. It's a place of connection.

Food feeds not only our bodies, but our souls as well. **John 6:35** tells us that Jesus is the bread of life.
1 Corinthians 3:16-17 & 19-20 tell us that our bodies are holy, it is the temple, and because our bodies are the temple of the Holy Spirit, we should take care of our bodies not only physically, but more importantly, spiritually. We must always be mindful of what we feed our temples.
In **Deuteronomy 8:10,** the Lord also reminds us that when we have eaten our fill, we must give thanks to the Lord.

Have you ever noticed that when we are stressed, some of us reach for food? It's one of the first places we run to – the kitchen. Maybe that's where the term "Comfort Food" comes from.

The Kitchen

The kitchen is the place we run to in times of pain, sadness, and the issues of life.

We ponder over a cup of tea or coffee, or some unhealthy food.

We call and invite our best friend or a neighbor, or a sibling. The person we feel we can trust to discuss what the issue is, and we make that pot of tea or coffee, and rehash what our problems are. We sit thoughtfully and ponder our next move; we probably cry to that person, sometimes we also cry out to the Lord, and talk to Him.

The kitchen can also be the busiest place in the home, a place of distractions. Just like the heart, a part of the body that is most important, we need to be careful with what we feed it, and who resides in it.

Just as some foods are unhealthy, and we stay away from unhealthy foods, we must also be mindful of what we put into our spiritual bodies.
Do we feed our spiritual bodies with unforgiveness, hate, anger, bitterness, and jealousy, just to name a few?

In talking to God, seeking His face, and reading His word, our kitchens and pantries can be filled with Love, Peace, Joy, and Forgiveness.
If we are not mindful of what is in our spiritual kitchens, the next place the Lord would take us to is the Stove – the fire of refining!

The Stove

The Stove is used for cooking. To cook, it needs heat.

Webster has the meaning of Stove as an apparatus that generates heat for special purposes. When God has a special purpose for our lives, we must go through this process which is the fire (**Daniel 3:16-25**). **Isaiah 48:10** tells us of our refining process. It is not always a good place or season for us. We certainly don't enjoy these seasons of refining and isolation, but they are necessary seasons in our lives if we are to become what Christ wants us to be and to fulfill His plans and purposes for our lives. Rest assured, His protective hands are upon us, and He is always with us during this process. He may be silent, but that is all part of His plan.

This is so that we draw close to Him and build a deeper relationship with Him.

Always remember that God uses these refining/heating moments to build our faith, increase our faith levels, and draw closer to Him so that ultimately, we can be used by Him.

Our refining moments or seasons are where God uses the fire to cleanse us, purify us, mold us, reshape us, refine us so that we would be without spot, wrinkle, and blemish. That's the church He's coming back for (**Ephesians 5:27**).

Just as some foods need to be roasted over a hot pit, the hot pit or fiery furnace is where Christ's power is displayed, not our own.

If we can handle everything in our own strength and ability, we will not see God's keeping power or Glory.

Ultimately, all power and glory belong to God and God alone!

The Pantry

Oxford says that the meaning of Pantry is a small room or closet in which food, dishes and utensils are kept.

The name Pantry was derived from the Middle English "panetrie" from the early French panetier – "servant in charge of food storage" from pan – bread (Wikipedia).

The Pantry is a reminder of God's abundant provision. Looking into my pantry as I write, it is interesting to see the shelves lined with various cans, bottles, boxes, and bags of foodstuff. All organized and ready to be used to make something delightful.

Likewise, our Spiritual Pantry is our prayer closet – our storage room or secret room where we commune with God, and we store God's word in our spiritual pantries. God's word is like the ingredients we use, like a can of fasting when in the fiery furnace. When we are in the various seasons of abundance, we take out the bottles of praise and worship ingredients. God bottles our tears (**Psalm 56:8**). This was David's way of saying that we can trust in God as He sees our pain.

We need ingredients/God's word to go through the process of refinement. Jesus will always be our Chef.

Always remember that when we go to Him in our trials and tribulations, the ingredients in our pantries are what He will use to guide us. This means that we must ensure that our pantries are well-stocked with all the right ingredients, which is His word, and His word does not expire!

God's word has no expiration date, whereas the foods of the flesh and what we eat all have expiration dates.

Just as we go directly to recipe books to get recipes and the ingredients needed for those favorite recipes, it's the same with God. We go to the Bible for spiritual ingredients for all our issues of life. When we are making our favorite foods, we must have all the ingredients, or the dish is compromised.

When our spiritual pantries have limited ingredients, it limits what God has to use to work with. Not that He can't use what we have, but we will be compromised, and our full potential won't be used for His honor and Glory. Spoilage is guaranteed.

By failing to read and study God's word consistently, our ingredients are limited, which means that instead of being able to enjoy a huge banquet, we may only be able to enjoy a meal for one.

Kitchen Utensils

There are various and numerous types of kitchen utensils. We have cutlery, cooking utensils, and various categories of utensils.
My focus will be on the ones that God laid on my heart that connect with Him and His word.

POTS

We use these vessels to cook. Pots come in various shapes and sizes. Depending on how far we want to go, our willingness and obedience to God, and to be used by God, will depend on our pot size. The levels and depths of the anointing will dictate how deep our pots will be.

Spiritually, we are God's vessels to be used by Him. Our vessels should always be vessels of honor, filled with the Holy Spirit and the fruit of the Spirit.
Our "pots" must be sanctified and useful to our Chef Jesus.
Some pots need to be seasoned before use; God must clean and prepare us to be used.
He can only use our vessels if they are cleaned.
What are we putting in our spiritual pots?
Our pots must be cleaned and seasoned so that they can be used to transform and hold something that is far greater than we can think or imagine.

God is so great, always remember He can also fix broken pots. That's His business. To heal that which is broken (**Psalm 147:3 & Jeremiah 18:1-4**). The potter and the clay. Even if we are marred, He can make us again into another vessel, one that He can use.

These various-sized pots also resemble the level of our faith in Christ. We are all given a measure of faith (**Romans 12:3**). But is it enough for everything that happens in our lives? Is it enough to carry us through our seasons of famine?
It is our responsibility to grow our faith so that we can stand and fight against all that the devil throws at us.

Some pots are shallow, like frying pans and sauté pans. These represent ankle-deep faith, as with most of us, which is almost no faith. This faith comes from a lack of understanding of God and His word. **Matthew 16:8**. That kind of faith shows up as worrying (which is a robber of faith), fear, doubt, and anxiety. **Matthew 8:25-26 & Matthew 14:31.**

Pots

The saucepan is the knee-deep faith. This is a weak kind of faith. We are reactive to situations, and our emotions, or rather our flesh, react before we can exercise our faith. **James 2:26** reminds us that faith without works is dead.

The double boilers and the soup pots are much deeper. They represent a strong faith. This is what I call "in over my head" faith. This is faith where we have no control over our negative situations and have to completely surrender our will to God. Regardless of my circumstances, I, without a doubt, believe that God will do what He has promised, despite what I see, despite what is happening, He is more than able. **Romans 4:20-21.**
Without faith, it is impossible to please Him. Faith is not crying and pleading. It is taking God at His word, His promises to us, as His children.

The Spoon

Spoons and ladles are the two pieces of utensils that are used to hold food. A spoon represents the act of serving. It also signifies humility. Just as a spoon feeds us, we are called to feed and serve others selflessly, before our fleshly desires.

In **John 21:15-17**, Jesus asks Peter if he loves Him to feed His sheep. This means that Peter needs to preach the gospel and spread the word of God.

Let us approach each day with hearts willing to serve and nourish those in need, just as God cares for us.

Like pots, spoons come in various sizes. Ladles hold more than regular spoons. How much of God, His ways, and His word are we holding to serve?

Spoons are also used to measure, so the same measure we give is the same measure that comes back. **Luke 6:38**.

In **Exodus 25:29**, the people were told to make spoons, dishes, covers, and bowls of Gold. In **Numbers 4:7**, upon the table spread a cloth of blue and put the dishes, spoons, bowls, and covers.

Throughout the scriptures, some vessels were used and were very symbolic. The spoon was used to burn incense.

The Knife

A knife is a cutting instrument and can also be used as a weapon.

Spiritually, a knife signifies severing, as in cutting away unwanted parts of our lives. God spiritually wants to prune us and remove the weeds of our lives **John 15:6.**

In a chef's kit, it is the most important tool. Knives vary by type and are made for various uses.

As a cutting instrument, a knife is used to cut various foods or to pare fruit.

Spiritually, it is used for cutting the darkness of sin. The knife has a dual purpose. It is used for cutting and pruning our sinful nature, or can be used as a weapon.

One of the most symbolic ways the knife was supposed to be used was in Abraham's sacrifice and obedience. His faith was tested when God asked him to sacrifice his only son – Isaac in **Genesis 22:1-14**.

In **Proverbs 22:18**, God speaks about us speaking without thinking. That our words cut like a knife.

In **Matthew 5:29-30**, Jesus cautions us about sin and if our right hand is causing us to sin, to cut it off and throw it away. Even though it was not meant to do so literally, what Jesus is warning us to do is to avoid what causes us to sin; we must separate ourselves from it, and this includes relationships.

Bowls/Dishes

A bowl is a round dish generally used for preparing, serving, and storing food.
Back in those days, even today, bowls were and are used for holding food, water, and other items.

Bowls are very symbolic. It suggests unity, especially among some communities. When invited to someone's home, some people carry a bowl or dish of food for "sharing". When someone passes, neighbors, friends, and family can be seen bringing dishes of food.
In **Revelation 16:1,** God instructs seven angels to pour seven bowls of wrath on Earth. This wrath will be poured out on the Earth for its idolatry.
What are our spiritual bowls storing or holding? How are we preparing our bowls to be of service in God's kingdom?
Our bowls should also have the capacity to hold our blessings.

Methods of Cooking

There are a few methods of cooking that are used, and I will compare them to how God operates.

There is the fast Microwave method, the Slow Cooking process, and the Deep Frying. In researching these cooking methods, I immediately understood why God prefers the latter two. Oh, to God be the Glory! Revelation just dawned on me while writing about the methods!

When God says yes, whether it's a microwave yes or a slow cooking yes, we must always be mindful that He has our best interest at heart. It will never be His wish to see us perish! (**2 Peter3:9**). He loves us very much.
When He says no or not yet, it means that we are not ready or mature to handle our blessings. His blessings are to make us rich and add no sorrow to it (**Proverbs 10:22**). He also wants us to be thankful in that which is least, the small blessings. When we are thankful for the small blessings and have an attitude of gratitude, then He knows that He can trust us with the abundance, the huge blessings!
(**Matthew 25:23**)

An outright no is His way of saying that it is not in our best interest. There is something better and more deserving. An example of this is in praying for a relationship to be restored. If it was a relationship that destroyed us as a person, maybe abusive, but because we see ourselves as underserving or not good enough, or with poor self-esteem, we think it's what we deserve. God says as His child we deserve so much better. Part of this comes from His healing us emotionally and deliverance. He says He is close to the broken-hearted (**Psalm 34:18**).

Methods of Cooking

Microwave

This is a kitchen appliance that cooks food by passing electromagnetic waves through it. Heat results from the absorption of energy by the water molecules in the food. This is a very fast way of cooking.

Most times when we pray, we want God to microwave the answers. We don't want to wait for the answer. We need and want it now, immediately! God does not operate in this way.

God answers in 'Yes, No,' I have something better, and there is always a waiting period, and that is coupled with obedience.

He is a God of Yes and Amen through and only through His word.

When we pray His word, which are His promises (**2 Corinthians 1:20**) we pray His word back to Him, and He honors His word to His Glory. Be reminded that His answers are also wrapped in obedience.

God is not a microwave God, especially if what we are asking for will destroy us in the end. It will destroy us because we may not be mature enough to handle what we ask for. I am reminded when James and John's mother asked for her two sons to be given that place on either side of Jesus (**Matthew 20:20-28**) Jesus told her that she had no idea of what she was asking for. Were they able to take the suffering He was about to take.

He sees the big picture; He knows the end from the beginning (**Isaiah 46:9-19**).

This is not to say there will not be moments or times when we will get those microwave answers.

Crockpot or Slow Cooking

If you were to ask me, I believe this is God's favorite way of "cooking"! I smile at this because I have been and am still going through His slow-cooking method. It is such a perfect analogy for how God perfects us.

Slow cooking is a method used to cook food over a very long period of time. Ironically, normally, large or tougher cuts of meat are cooked this way. This process or technique ensures that all the flavor goes in gradually. The heat is at a low simmering heat.

God uses this process for some of us, maybe because we are tough and not pliable to Him. He wants us to humble ourselves.

For us to develop the fruit of the Holy Spirit, we need to be broken down so we can fulfill our purpose.

He will slow cook us by allowing us to face life's challenges, trials, and tribulations until we are ready for service in His kingdom. The slow cooking method dates back to **Genesis 25**.

This was how Jacob cooked his lentils and stew. The Bible said that it was delectable!

If we want to be flavorful/fruitful in God's kingdom, the slow cooking process is the way we must go; there are no shortcuts when it comes to the Kingdom of God.

The slow-cooking process comes with a waiting period, also.

Our obedience and what we do in that waiting period also determines our fruitfulness, or in cooking analogy, our flavors!

Deep Frying

Deep frying is the process of cooking foods by submerging them in extremely hot oil until they reach the required internal temperature.

We must periodically check the internal temperature by inserting a food thermometer. Deep frying is fast, but it has its dangers.

Deep frying, when done properly, destroys the bacteria.

In the Old Testament, we see fire was used for burnt offerings as a way of repentance, as an offering to God.

The act of repentance is just like what happens in the deep-frying process. Bacteria are destroyed. In our deep-frying process, our fleshly desires are destroyed.

When we no longer walk in the flesh, God can use us as we are free from "Bacteria".

Biblically, fire is used many times. It represents the presence of the Holy Spirit as we see in **Acts 2:3-4** on the day of Pentecost.

God appeared to Moses as a burning bush **Exodus 3:2**. He guided the Israelites by a pillar of fire by night when they were fleeing Egypt (**Exodus 13:20-22**).

He uses fire to refine us, **Zechariah 13:9 and Malachi 3:2** speak of God being like a refiner's fire.

Paul, in **1 Corinthians 3:12-15** writes about how our works or deeds will be tested by fire, burning away what is not of God in us.

We see so many illustrations in the Bible of the all-consuming fire, how it processes gold, and how anything of value must go through the fire process.

Creativity

Creativity is the use of the imagination or original ideas, especially in artistic work.
Research by (Forketers.com), this is where science and art come together. A chef must come out of his comfort zone and create.
Just as God is the Creator. The very first act in the Bible was the creation of the world and man.

If you look at meals coming out of top restaurants, the food looks so pretty and well presented. You can see that presentation is especially important. I often watch the Food Network Shows like Top Chef, Master Chef, etc., and some of them have very bold personalities.
Presenting food with precision is important.

With God, He demands sometimes that we be bold, as He said in **1 Timothy 1:7-8**, He tells us to pray with boldness, expecting our prayers to be answered.
God wants us to be with the same attribute towards Him.
How we present ourselves to Him, by being precise with our prayers, and not praying amiss.
Our prayers are also creative when we personalize His word back to Him. This reminds Him of His promise to us. We ought to pray His word back to Him.
Just as we create delightful meals in the kitchen, we must also create an atmosphere for the presence of God.

Creativity brings to mind baking and decorating a cake.
When they are making the decorations for the cake, the room must be clean, the atmosphere and temperature must be right for the cake not to fall, and for the icing to go on the cake without running. The consistency must be perfect.
Presentation is of utmost importance, so too we must present ourselves as a living sacrifice to The Lord, Holy and pleasing to God (*Romans 12:1*)
Our body is the temple of the Holy Spirit and must be clean, with the right ingredients, which are the fruit of the Holy Spirit.

Recipe for Sponge Cake:

Ingredients:
6 large eggs (room Temperature)
1 cup granulated sugar
1 cup all-purpose Flour
½ tsp baking Powder

Preheat oven to 350°F

Instructions:
In a deep bowl, beat the eggs for 1 minute on high speed. Gradually add sugar and beat for 8-10 minutes, until fluffy and thick.
Whisk in flour and baking powder, then fold into the egg mixture with a spatula. Stop when all the flour is incorporated. Do not overmix or you will deflate the batter.
Pour into a lined baking pan.
Bake at 350°F for 25 minutes.
Remove from the pan and cool on a wire rack.

God's Recipe for Sponge Cake:

We must be like a Sponge, soaking in His word.
1 Cup Honey – Feel the sweetness of His presence, His holiness.
1 Cup Worship - Worship is like the flour, the ingredient that brings it together.
1 Cup Faith - Even if it's ½ a teaspoon, it's still bigger than a mustard seed.
Baked with the Fire of the Holy Spirit.
How long should we stay baking in the Fire of the Holy Spirit? Until we get the release through deliverance.

Passion

What is Passion? Webster defines it as: A strong feeling or emotion.

With passion comes challenging work and determination. A chef puts in long hours before the sun is up to late at night. You can only be successful if you put in the demanding work!

That desire and wanting to be successful helps develop the skill and precision needed. Your own personal techniques are what define your uniqueness as a chef. This is what carries you all the way to the top with success.

So too we must have a passion for God, a passion for the presence of God, and all things pertaining to God. (**Psalm 116:1**)
When we spend that quality time on our knees, on our faces. Sometimes in the wee hours of the morning. That defines us as a Child of God.
God requires that we spend that time with Him, in His presence. He will talk to us through His word, through a man or woman of God. When He speaks, He will always confirm His word.
We worship, we pray, we fast, and we develop the gifts of the Holy Spirit that has been given to us. We also develop the Fruit of the Spirit. But it takes passion and dedication to God. We must run after God (**Psalm 42:1**). Just as a deer pants for water, so our souls must pant after God. He wants all of us, meaning He wants all of you. Not part, not some, as He is a jealous God.

Just as a chef develops his skill and talent, so also, we develop our gifts. Whether it is healing, prophecy, wisdom, word of knowledge, faith, tongues, the interpretation of tongues, and working of miracles. (*1 Corinthians 13:7-11*).
Having a passion for God means we must go after the things of God and not our fleshly desires. (**Galatians 5:16-17**)

Recipe for Passion Fruit Mousse:

Ingredients:
3 Tbs water
1 1/3 cup of Heavy Cream (cold)
1 can of sweetened condensed milk
1 cup passion Fruit pulp
2 tsps unflavored gelatin (Optional)

Instructions:

Combine all ingredients in a blender for 5 minutes.
Transfer to a large serving bowl or small individual ramekins and refrigerate for 3 hours or overnight to set.

Leaving out the gelatin will result in a softer consistency. Gelatin gives a more solid consistency.

God's Recipe for Passion Fruit Mousse:

Mousse is composed of ingredients that are whipped until it is light and creamy. It is through being "whipped" that we become the man or woman that God calls us to be. It's called Trials & Tribulations. Whom the Lord loves, He chastens (**Hebrews 12:6**).
Heavy cream is the thick part of milk that rises to the top. We can only rise to the top by staying in His presence.
Condensed milk is when water has been taken out from the milk and a high concentration of sugar is added. What must we have removed from within us? Pride? Lust? Envy? Jealousy? How much of what is in us spiritually must be removed? Bad language, bad behavior, lack of morals, unforgiveness, and a bad attitude towards others, just to name a few.

Passion fruit has seeds and pulp; to get the fruit, it must be blended and strained. So. we too must be crushed and strained for us to be the fruit that God wants from us.

1 Cup of His Presence
1 Can of Sweet Worship
1 Cup of Fruit of the Spirit - Faithfulness
Unlike gelatin which is optional we need Faith so it can solidify and have a great texture!
Blend it all together until we become light and free from baggage.

Not a Lone Wolf

Being a Lone Wolf is likened to being a one-man show.
There are a couple of sayings about this. No man is an island; there is no I in Team.

The most powerful word against the Lone Wolf personality is when God says in **Matthew 18:19** If two of you agree as touching anything that they shall ask, it shall be done by my Father which is in heaven.

Being a Lone Wolf means that there is a bit of selfishness; you want all the glory for yourself, you don't want to share the spotlight, that's the spirit of pride. And God hates pride.
Sometimes in a work environment, there would always be that person who does not share information. They want all the accolades. That person carries a spirit of pride.
There are others that do not like to teach if you ask them how something should be done. That person carries some insecurities.

Granted, there are times that God puts you into the wilderness for a season, but that is because He wants you to build your relationship with Him. Even in that wilderness, you are not alone because He is always with us!

In the restaurant world, every chef in the kitchen has a role, and each role is important.
A chef can prepare the food, but what good is it if it remains in the pan? When the food is plated by another and he leaves it there, how would the customer get it?
We are all part of a giant puzzle, and when one piece is missing, the puzzle is not good.

In a kitchen, you will never be alone, just as God also promises throughout His word, that He will never leave us or forsake us. **Hebrews 13:5**.
All must work together as a team, just as the body of Christ must come together.
As He says in **Psalm 133:1** How good it is for the brethren to dwell together in unity. It is like precious oil poured on the head.
Hebrews 10:25 Not forsaking the assembling of ourselves together.

All recipes can be made by only one person. But in the restaurant environment, it takes many hands. Many hands are needed, as we must shop for the produce, prepare the ingredients – cut up, season, etc. before we cook.
If you look at even the street food cooks, you have the cook, the person who assembles the dish, and the person who bags and handles the money.
We can never be a Lone Wolf and be successful.

15 Minute Lo Mein Recipe

Ingredients:

8oz Lo Mein egg noodles
1 tbsp olive Oil
2 cloves of garlic minced
½ cup snow peas

2 cups mushrooms
1 red bell pepper
1 carrot

Sauce:

2 tbs soy sauce
1 tsp sesame Oil
½ tsp sriracha

2 tsp Sugar
½ tsp Ground Ginger

Carrots and bell peppers must be julienne style
Mushrooms sliced, snow peas whole.

Put all the ingredients for the sauce in a small bowl and whisk. Set aside.
Boil the egg noodles according to package instructions.

Instructions:

Heat oil in a large wok, over high heat. Add garlic, mushrooms, bell peppers, and carrots. Stir often until tender 3-4 minutes.
Stir in snow peas and stir for 2-3 minutes more.
Add the egg noodles and the sauce, combine, and remove from the heat.

God's Lo Mein Recipe:

Ingredients:

½ tsp Anointing Oil
1 Cup Faith

1 Prayer Partner
1 Cup of God's Word

Instructions:

Anoint yourselves and come into agreement with prayer and supplication. Standing in Faith on His word.
Cooking Temperature: He refines us, but not as Silver, He tests us in the Furnace of affliction. All for His Glory and honor. **Isaiah 48:10-11**

Daniel 1:12 & 15 – *Daniel, Hananiah, Mishael, and Azariah ate vegetables for ten days. Their features appeared better, and they were fatter in flesh. Meaning their skin was healthy.*

Grace Under Fire

In the world of cooking, this means that we must remain cool and calm under pressure. The kitchen must always have a spirit of camaraderie with each other.

In God's kitchen, we must be under affliction, under testing, trials, and tribulation, stay in His presence, stay in worship, stand in faith believing that when we come out of this heat, we will be perfected. As He says, He will perfect that which concerns us. **Psalm 138:8**

Grace is a gift from God. It is the unmerited favor of God, the Divine love of God, even when we don't deserve it.
We see the Grace of God throughout the bible.
As *Living by Design* aptly describes it, in **John 1:17** the law was given to Moses, but grace and truth came through Jesus.
The Old Testament is about the law, and the New Testament is about Grace.
2 Timothy 1:9 explains that Jesus saved us, not by what we have done, but by His purpose and Grace.
God's Grace is the foundation of life.
When you ask some people how they are, and how are they doing, you often hear: "It's by God's grace!" that we are okay.
We see many examples of Grace in the bible.
Noah found Grace in the eyes of the Lord, **Genesis 6:8.**
Joseph was a perfect example, sold into slavery, wrongfully accused, but by God's Grace, his perspective was that God sent him ahead to prepare the way for his family. That is Grace!
Moses was stubborn, doubtful, and arrogant; he was a murderer, but God graciously used him despite his flawed personality. He guided him to lead the Israelites out of Egypt.
David, an adulterer, stole someone's wife, put a hit out on her husband, and lied, yet he received God's Favor. In fact, God said that David was a man after His own heart!
Could this be why David had to spend time in the wilderness and wrote so many of the Psalms? Seventy-five, to be exact, even though seventy-three bear his name.
Was that his testing season?

Many great men and women in the Bible were flawed, but God's Grace was upon them, where they were used to carry out the work of God.
His amazing Grace, how sweet that sound.

Garlic Butter Steak Recipe:

Ingredients:

2 tbsp Butter
½ tsp minced garlic
¾ lb top Sirloin steak
1/8 tsp black pepper

1 tsp freshly minced parsley
¼ tsp soy sauce
1/8 Tsp Salt

Instructions:
Mix butter, parsley, and garlic
Sprinkle the steak with salt and pepper on both sides.
Heat a large skillet to 400°F.
Sear the steak for 4-7 minutes on each side. This depends on a medium to well-done steak.
Searing the steak seals in the juices also. To accomplish this, you must not keep turning the steak.
Leave it to cook for the required time on each side.
Let the meat rest after cooking.

God's Recipe for Garlic Butter Steak:

Ingredients:
Arrogance   Salt
Rebellion   Grace

Instructions:
1 Samuel 2:3 – Boast no more so very proudly, do not let arrogance come out of your mouth, For the Lord is a God of knowledge and His actions are weighed.
1 Samuel 15:23 – Rebellion is as the sin of witchcraft. When we reject God, so too will He reject us.
James 4:6 He gives more grace to the humble when we submit to Him.
Matthew 5:13 – We are the salt of the earth; but if it loses its flavor, then it is good for nothing and should be thrown out.

Cooking Temperature: In Arrogance and Rebellion, we shall certainly be put into a fiery furnace until it is no longer a part of us if we are to be living in Grace.
We will be in that heat until we are sealed in the Blood of Jesus.

Take Criticism

Not everyone is going to like your food. We all have different palates.
Just as when you are in Christ, not everyone is going to like you.
The Pharisees did not like Jesus. Some Pharisees were won over, but some continued to criticize Him to the very end.
We all still must learn and take criticism constructively if we are to succeed.
Choose to learn from it, choose to try to be better.

Chefs are always changing their recipes and techniques to be the best in their culinary game.
They see criticism as an opportunity to adjust the recipes.
We must always be willing to change. We cannot expect different results by doing the same thing the same way.

Criticism is judging. Judging others. People who judge do this out of an issue they have within themselves.
Matthew 7:1-5 says Do not judge so that we will not be judged. The same standard we measure will be the same measure we will be measured. Take the plank out of our eye instead of the speck in the other's eye.

Some people are super sensitive when someone criticizes them. Some are thin-skinned, so they take it negatively, some are thick-skinned and just do not care.
Whilst constructive criticism is good, we should be mindful not to hurt the other person. When we hurt, then it is not constructive.
Some people criticize out of envy and jealousy. Some out of being malicious.
That is not constructive, and it can destroy a person. A true friend or boss, or someone close to you will give constructive criticism. When it is constructive, they will share the negative and balance it with double the positive.
God does not criticize or condemn us. He loves us, and we must emulate that quality of holding each other up. He throws our sins into the sea of forgetfulness. **Micah 7:19**

Good chefs turn criticism into learning and making their recipes better.

Wisdom is listening to constructive criticism, rejecting it is Pride, and you only do yourself an injustice.
Do not turn it into a personal war; sometimes we must choose our battles to win the war.

Harvard Business Review says that "Critics are often intelligent, talented, and productive". Unfortunately, these traits can be used to disparage others.

Note: *Everyone hates critics, so I chose a food that most people hate – Anchovy*

Recipe for Anchovy Sauce:

Ingredients:
2 cans anchovy in Olive Oil
¼ tsp thyme
3 tbsp red wine vinegar
Black pepper to taste.

2 cloves of garlic
1 ½ tbsp Dijon mustard
2 cups virgin olive oil

Instructions:
Blend all ingredients except olive oil in a food processor, puree for 1 minute
While the processor is running slowly, add the olive oil until the mixture is thick and smooth.
A little goes a long way, so use sparingly.

God's Recipe for Anchovy Sauce:

Ingredients:
1 Cup Humility
1 Cup Anointing Oil

1 Cup kindness
1 Cup of Love

Instructions:
Mix them together until you get a Spirit of Compassion.

Cooking Temperature: **James 4:6** God opposes the proud but gives Grace to the humble.

Detail Oriented

Attention to detail is a part of life for a chef. From choosing his ingredients to presentation of the food, this is extremely critical.

Plating and presentation require a chef to be a perfectionist; food preparation, plating, and presentation must have a chef's undivided attention.

His attention to detail must be perfect.

Just as a chef, God pays attention to every detail of our lives. He perfects that which concerns us. (**Psalm 138:8**).

In **Matthew 22:14**, Jesus says that many are called but few are chosen. What does this mean? Jesus calls us to follow Him because He loves us. But how many of us are willing to go through the trials and tribulations for us to be perfected in Him?

How much of our attention does He get? The chosen are the ones who will walk through fire for Him.

For us to prepare for the second coming of Christ, our lives must be perfected, and every detailed area of our lives must glorify Him.

Romans 12:1 says that we must present our bodies as a living sacrifice, holy and pleasing to God.

Taking each part of our bodies to make it a living sacrifice means that my feet should not go where angels fear to tread or where God will not go, but run to where I can be of service to God.

My Arms should not be used to take selfishly or be used to do evil, but be lifted in continuous praise.

My tongue must not be used to speak evil, but for the speaking of the word of God, and on God's behalf.

Just as a chef transforms his ingredients into a perfect dish, so too must our lives be transformed to God's will and way.

Recipe for Puffs:
Ingredients:

½ cup of water	8 tbsp unsalted butter
1 tsp granulated sugar	¼ tsp salt
1 cup Flour	4 eggs (room temperature)

Instructions:

In a saucepan, combine the butter, water, salt, and sugar and bring to a boil, using medium heat.
Remove from the heat and stir in all the flour at once with a wooden spoon.
Once the flour is incorporated, place on the medium heat, stirring constantly for 2 minutes.
The dough will be smooth and come together as a ball.
Preheat the oven to 350°F

Let this cool so that you can add the eggs. Be careful, as you don't want the eggs to cook.
Add the eggs one at a time. Do not add another egg until the first egg is completely incorporated into the dough mixture.
Put the dough mix into a piping bag using a ½" round tip. Pipe 30 puffs, leaving space between them.
Place it in the oven and bake for 25 minutes, until golden brown.
Important: *Do not shake the oven or open the oven door before they are finished. This can cause the puffs to fall.*

God's Puff Recipe:

Ingredients:

1 Cup Worship	1 Cup Fasting
1 Cup Faith	1 Cup of Bible Reading

Instructions:
Mix all ingredients and place in a bowl of Trials & Tribulations

Temperature: Bake until perfected.

Puffs are temperamental; you cannot leave them in the oven too long, nor can you take them out before their time. They will deflate. The timing must be perfect. Just as God's timing is not ours, His timing is perfect!

Endurance & Stamina

A chef's life entails challenging work. They are on their feet from sun-up until the wee hours of the morning.

They must manage the staff with the day's food preparations.

There may be ingredients to buy at the market. If the kitchen staff does not show up, they must fill that role. They must also oversee what the team is doing. Even if you do have an effective team, consistency in the food you serve, takes effective management of your team.

Chefs cannot become complacent. Not everyone has a good day, but they must still function.

Spending long hours on your feet can be particularly challenging. Chefs must be physically prepared for the long hours.

When we are in Christ, we also need to spend hours travailing before Him, whether it's on our knees or on our faces. If we are to learn about Him, we must spend those hours in His presence, fasting and praying, seeking Him.

It is never easy trying to build a relationship with God. You will find yourself under attack until your faith is so strong that you can withstand those attacks.

With God, we have been tried many times in life. This is so He can move us to the next level in Him.

As we say, every level has a different devil. But He equips us with His word to endure.

As **Ecclesiastes 9:11** says, the race is not for the swift, but for those who can endure.

I love the description in **Hebrews 10:36** – For you have need of endurance, so that when you have done the will of God, you may receive His promises.

Webster describes stamina as having the mental or bodily ability to sustain a prolonged, stressful effort.

Well may I tell you, when we are in Christ, we must go through prolonged trials. Joseph's trials lasted thirteen years. What carried Joseph was that he never gave up on the dream that God gave him.

In **2 Corinthians 12:9,** He promises His power is made perfect in our weakness.

So, when chefs must be on their feet for long hours, God tells us in **1 Corinthians 16:13** to be watchful, stand firm in the faith, act like men, be strong.

Recipe for Beef Stew:

Ingredients:

2lbs beef cut into 1" pieces
½ tsp salt
1 clove of garlic minced
1 tsp paprika
1 onion chopped
1 tbsp oil

¼ cup flour
½ tsp black pepper
1 bay leaf
1 tsp Worcestershire sauce
1 ½ cups beef broth
2 tbsp brown sugar

Instructions:
Put all ingredients except beef broth, oil, and brown sugar into a bowl and mix. Pour over the meat and marinate for 1 hour.

Cooking Temperature: Heat a skillet and add oil, then put the brown sugar into the oil. When it starts to get a golden-brown color, add the meat. Transfer into a crock pot. Keep stirring until the meat is seared. Add the beef broth and turn the heat to low and cook for 10-12 hours, or you can cook on medium heat for 4-6 hours.

God's Recipe for Beef Stew:

Ingredients:

1 Cup Courage
1 Tbsp Faith
1 ½ Tbsp Prayer

1 Cup Strength
1 Tbsp Fasting
1 Cup Worship

Instructions:
Mix Prayer and Fasting with Worship and Faith.

Cooking Temperature: Slow cooking over low heat to get the courage and strength needed to face your battles.

A Leader

What makes a great leader?

According to *Adam Enfroy*, the most important qualities a leader should have are Integrity, Accountability, Empathy, Humility, Vision, Influence, and Positivity.

The top five characteristics of a leader are: Integrity, Ability to delegate, Communication, Gratitude, and Empathy. These are what define you as a leader.

Great leaders help people reach their goals, and they are not afraid to hire people who are better than they are. Great leaders celebrate your accomplishments. They are mentors, they are trustworthy.

Having spent many years in management, I found it necessary and important to push those on my team to accomplish and do better. To set ambitious standards for them. It was not always received in a positive manner, and I know that there were times my way was a bit harsh, but I always told them not to take it personally, it is because I love them and want better for them, to see them grow and become successful.

As a leader, you should always recognize hidden talent and potential. I made sure training and development were part of their employment. It is not in the interest of a leader to hold back those under them. A great leader should have a very clear vision not only for his or herself but also for those under their stewardship. That is what sets you apart and defines you as a leader.

As a chef, a good leader must oversee the staff, motivate them, train them, and develop them. As a leader, a chef must also manage stock, menus, and be on top of the financials.

What does God say about leadership?

In **Titus 1:7-14**, it says that a leader must be an overseer, be God's steward, and be above reproach. A leader must not be arrogant, quick-tempered, or greedy for gain, but be hospitable, love doing good, have self-control, must have integrity, be upright, Holy, and disciplined.

1 Timothy 3:2 puts it all concisely: an overseer must be above reproach, sober-minded, self-controlled, respectable, hospitable, and able to teach.

A leader having those qualities and characteristics is one whom God will always prosper.

Too many leaders today are missing those qualities and characteristics. It is all about financial gain, and workers are suffering at their hands. No empathy is given to the employees.

When God gives you a mandate and puts you in the role to lead, lead by example, as you must give an account in the end.

Matthew 23:11 says: The greatest among you shall be your servant.

Jesus was first a servant.

Recipe for Lamb Chops Sizzled with Garlic:

*Ingredients***:**

8 ½" thick lamb chops
Dried thyme
10 small Garlic cloves (Halved)
2 tbsp fresh lemon juice
Crushed red pepper

Salt & ground pepper
3 tbsp extra virgin olive oil
3 tbsp water
2 tbsp minced parsley

Instructions:
Season the lamb with salt and pepper, and sprinkle the thyme over both sides.
In a large skillet, heat oil until shimmering. Add the lamb chops and garlic and cook over moderately high heat, until both sides are browned, about 3 minutes each side. Plate.
Leave garlic in skillet, and add water, lemon juice, parsley, and crushed red pepper to pan and cook 1 minute. Pour over the lamb and serve.

God's Recipe for Lamb Chops Sizzled with Garlic:

Ingredients:
1 Cup Integrity
1 Cup Love

2 Cups Self-Control
3 Cups of servanthood

Instructions:
Mix ingredients until you see empathy and vision forming.

Cooking Temperature: Sizzle in skillet until it forms into a Leader

Defined Palate

Something I have always admired is when you see a chef tasting a dish and can name the ingredients in that dish. He can tell every spice or ingredient that is present.

Some of the Top Chef shows have as part of the competition, spice testing, where the chefs must be blindfolded and guess the name of the spices. Not all get it perfectly correct, and they can only use the spices they guessed correctly!

As *Forketers* explain, a chef must taste and study a recipe, which requires concentration, so they are able to pick out the ingredients. They must discern what is cooking based on aroma and must have the gift of discernment for flavors and ingredients. Chefs must have trained minds and a good palate. This takes constant training and exercise to develop the skill.

Chefs develop this gift by practicing dark tasting, and the key is to remove distractions except for taste!

Key words and attributes that stood out that align with God's gifts and word are having the gift of discernment, aroma, removing distractions, and trained minds.

The Gift of **Discernment,** as explained in **1 Corinthians 12:10**; is a gift of the Holy Spirit. It is a revelation gift, and it is called the discerning of the spirits. God gives us discernment.

Sometimes you will hear someone say, "something told me." In fact, that's discernment that's kicking in. The Holy Spirit is moving in us. It can be a warning; it comes like a feeling. But when we are in tune with God and the Holy Spirit, when we have that relationship, then we will be quickened in our spirits.

Aroma, Ephesians 5:2 tells us to walk in love, just as Christ also loved us and gave Himself, as an offering and a sacrifice to God as a fragrant aroma.

Our worship must be a sweet-smelling aroma to God's nostrils for our breakthroughs, and our answers.

Distractions are like temptations. When Jesus wanted to pray, he removed Himself and went alone to avoid the noise and distractions. **Mark 1:35**

Romans 12:2 tells us: to not be conformed to this world, but be transformed by the renewal of the mind, that by testing, you may discern what is the will of God, what is good and acceptable and perfect.

Throughout the Bible, you see that when God wanted to build a relationship with anyone, He moved them into the wilderness. He was removing distractions from their lives. It's in our wilderness moments and seasons that we build a relationship with God. There is no one to distract us. To hear His whisper, we must lean in to hear!

That is what having the Defined Palate of God should be.

Recipe for Tika Masala Chicken:

Ingredients:

1 1/2lb boneless chicken thighs
2 tsp salt
2 tsp ground cumin
1 tsp smoked paprika
½ tsp black pepper
1/8 tsp ground cardamom
1 finely chopped onion
4 cloves garlic finely grated
1 cup crushed tomatoes
2 tbsp fresh cilantro
½ cup chicken broth

1 tbs oil
2 tsp garam masala
1 tsp ground coriander
1 tsp ground tumeric
¼ tsp cayenne pepper
2 tbsp ghee
¼ cup tomato paste
1 tbsp grated ginger
1 can coconut milk
½ tsp red pepper flakes

Instructions:

Coat the chicken with oil and mix in all the spices. Coat evenly and let marinate overnight or at least 45 minutes.

Melt ghee in a skillet and cook chicken thighs until browned 5-10 minutes. Transfer onto a plate. Reduce heat to medium-high, stir in onions until soft, 5 minutes, add tomato paste until it caramelizes, 5 minutes, stir in garlic and ginger, cook until fragrant, 1 minute.

Pour in crushed tomatoes and bring to a boil. Pour in coconut milk, chicken, and broth, bring to a simmer on low heat, and cook, stirring occasionally, until all the flavors are blended and the sauce is reduced. 15 minutes.

God's Recipe for Tika Masala Chicken:

Ingredients:

3 Cups of Worship
1 Cup Anointing Oil
1 Cup Discernment

3 Cups Love
1 Cup Blind Faith
2 Cups Prayer

Instructions:

Coat Discernment in Oil, Prayer, and Blind Faith.
Worship with Love, and slow cook until the fruit of the Spirit is developed.

Commitment

What exactly is commitment? *Oxford* explains it as being dedicated to. *Webster* has it as a promise to do or to give something.

A chef must be committed to success through the food they plate. Without a commitment to serving great food, there will be failure, and their restaurant will have to close its doors.

Commitment in a chef's life includes respect and having a great rapport with the team.

What does commitment mean spiritually?

Our commitment to God means, firstly, that we must be faithful to Him. We must have that depth of faithfulness, and it must also show in our attitudes and behavior, not only in our spiritual life but also in our physical lives.

We can only develop by our commitment to God's word. Commitment of the time we spend in His presence. Some people only commit to Him once a week for one hour!

That is not what He wants. He wants all of us, meaning my all, your all. Seeking Him in the morning, during the day, in the night.

Seek Him and commit everything that we do to Him daily!

We are committed to our families, our jobs, and the companies we work for, and our relationships.

When we commit to these things, we see that we are successful.

But how can we enjoy this success without our commitment to God first?

Psalm 37:5-6 says that we should commit everything we do to the Lord. Trust Him, and He would help us.

The word commit appears 164 times in the bible. So, it is an important ingredient in our Christian lives.

Proverbs 16:3 – Commit your work to the Lord, and your plans will be established.

Colossians 3:23 says – Whatever you do, work heartily, as for the Lord and not for men.

Paul and Ruth are just two examples of commitment.

Ruth was committed to Naomi. As we can see, this led to her marriage to Boaz.

Paul was committed to the Lord after his conversion from Saul to Paul.

The greatest act of commitment comes from the Lord. He is committed to us through His word.

If we follow Him in Spirit and in Truth. He watches over His word to perform it.

Recipe for Olive Bread:

Ingredients:

3 ½ cups of flour
1 pk active dry yeast
1 tbsp chopped fresh thyme
4 tbsp olive oil
½ cup chopped black olives
1 egg yolk beaten

1 tsp salt
1 tsp brown sugar
1 cup lukewarm water
½ cup chopped green olives
1 ¾ cups sliced sun-dried tomatoes

Instructions:

Mix yeast, sugar into lukewarm water, and let it proof for 10 minutes.
Mix flour, salt, and thyme. Make a well and pour in the yeast and oil. Knead until it leaves the sides of the bowl.
Turn out onto a lightly floured counter and knead in the olives and the tomatoes, knead for 5 minutes more, until the dough is smooth and elastic.

Brush a bowl with oil and place the dough. Cover with plastic and let it rise for 1 ½ hours or until doubled in size.
Punch down and cut in half, as this would give 2 loaves. Shape into loaves or ovals and place in the sheet pan or loaf tins. Place in a warm place to rise for 45 minutes.
Preheat oven to 400°F.
Make 3 diagonal slashes on the bread and brush with room temperature egg yolk.
Bake 40 minutes, until golden brown and the loaves sound hollow when tapped on the bottom.
Transfer to wire rack to cool.

God's Olive Bread Recipe:

Ingredients:

1 Cup Anointing Oil
1 Cup of Fasting
3 ½ Cups Prayer

1 Cup of Sweet Worship
1 Tbsp Salt of the Earth

Instructions:

Then cut off everything that does not belong in your life.
Make a well with the Prayer, and pour in the Fasting, Oil, Worship, and Salt.
Knead until it comes together, and your vessel is clean.
Bake in the Fire of the Holy Spirit. It is ready when the Fruits of the Spirit manifest.

Intuition

Intuition plays a vital role in a chef's life. They need to be quick thinkers.

As *Gourmetian* says, Intuition will lead the team through uncharted waters and keep them from sinking.

How often our lives are like this, and we need the Gift of Discernment. When I came across Intuition, I asked myself if it's not the same as discernment. Actually, it's not.

I understand now that Intuition is an immediate understanding based on feeling. Discernment is more scriptural and not based on a feeling. It's about thinking scripturally about all areas of our spiritual lives. Our lives, for us to have the gift of discernment, must be uncompromising.

Discernment is a vital part of a Christian's life, and we can only get this by spending quality time in prayer with God.

Wisdom is also required, and God tells us that when we lack wisdom, all we must do is ask and He will give us that wisdom liberally. That means He gives it freely! **James 1:5.**

Many times, when something is amiss, we say to others or even to ourselves, "my gut" or "something told me", or "I have a feeling".

This is the move of the Holy Spirit through the gift of Discernment.

The heart of Spiritual Discernment is being able to distinguish the voice of God from the voice of the world.

Jesus says that His sheep will know His voice, and they will follow Him. **John 10:27-28**

The Holy Spirit will always lead us through our uncharted waters. We have a divine plan and destiny to fulfil, and we need the direction and guidance of the Lord.

God also warns us to test the spirits because not every spirit is of God. **1 John 4:1**

All our journeys take us through uncharted waters. Our journeys will not always be smooth, but with Faith, Trust, and Discernment, we will make it into the promise that He gave us.

Just as He led Moses and the Israelites out of Egypt with a pillar of cloud by day and pillar of fire by night **Exodus 13:21-22,** so will He also lead us to where He wants us.

They were going through an uncharted journey, but had to trust God, for the GPS to reach the Promised Land.

We need to have Trust and faith that God will see us through. We must stay in His word and in His presence to keep from sinking.

This reminds me of Peter, angry with Jesus, because there was a terrible storm and Jesus was fast asleep in the boat. He even told Jesus that He did not care if they drowned. **Luke 8:22-25.**

Faith and trust will carry us through.

Recipe for Apricot Cobbler:

Ingredients:

¾ cup sugar

¼ tsp ground cinnamon

1 cup water

1 tbsp butter

1 tbsp cornstarch

1/8 tsp nutmeg

3 cans apricot halves

Topping:

1 cup flour

1 ½ tsp baking powder

3 tbsp cold butter

1 tbsp sugar

½ tsp salt

½ cup whole milk

Instructions:

In a saucepan, combine sugar, cinnamon, nutmeg, and cornstarch and stir in water until smooth. Bring to a boil over medium heat and stir for 1 minute. Reduce heat and add Apricots and butter. Pour into a shallow 2 qt baking dish.

Topping:

Combine flour, sugar, baking powder, and salt. Grate the butter into the flour mixture until crumbly. Stir in milk until moistened. Spoon over hot apricot mixture.

Bake at 400°F until golden brown, 30-35 minutesm and insert a toothpick into the topping. It must come out clean.

God's Apricot Cobbler Recipe:

Ingredients:

2 Cups Discernment

2 Cups Scriptures

½ Cup Worship

½ Tsp Salt

Instructions:

Combine all ingredients, mix until they all come together. On high heat, until it glows.

Topping:

God's Glory and His presence. Insert a trial and when you come out victorious, you are ready!

Mentorship

Great chefs and great leaders will never hold back anyone on their team. It's selfish, immature, and insecurity that encourages this behavior.

When you educate your team and encourage them to full potential, it says a great deal about you and your character and strength as a Leader.

Leadership and being a true leader are not always easy. You must accept responsibility.

Mentorship and Leadership carry the same qualities. The difference is that a mentor is a counselor or teacher.

Jesus mentored His disciples. They followed Him and gleaned from Him. He is a great teacher.

All of us are mentors in part, whether it be in our roles as Mothers, Fathers, Teachers, Employers, or a Coach, we are always in a mentorship position, mentoring someone.

Some people look to you as their mentor.

A mentor, in a nutshell, can be viewed as one who teaches.

In **Matthew 28:20,** Jesus tells His disciples to teach the people to observe everything He commanded.

In **John 14:26,** Jesus promised to send the Holy Spirit to teach us all things.

One of my favorite scriptures is from **Proverbs 27:17,** Iron sharpens iron, so one man sharpens another.

There were some great mentors in the Bible.

Elijah mentored Elisha, who was smart enough to ask for a double portion of his anointing. Nathan mentored David. Moses mentored Joshua. Eli mentored Samuel, who mentored both Saul and David.

Jesus mentored His disciples by imparting His knowledge on the difference between the values of the Kingdom of God and those of the world. What is important is that He taught by example, not just by words alone. Too many teach by words, not by example.

Paul was the best example of being a mentor. He said in **1 Corinthians 11:1** to follow his example as he followed the example of Christ.

Recipe for Grilled Quail with Pomegranate-Orange Sauce

Ingredients:

12 Quails. Remove backbones and bottom leg joints. Season with salt and black pepper, and lemon.

Pomegranate-Orange BBQ Sauce:

2 tbsp oil	1 small finely chopped onion	
1 cup pomegranate juice		
¼ cup orange Juice	¼ cup pomegranate molasses	¼ cup red wine vinegar
3 tbsps light brown sugar	2 cinnamon sticks	Zest of 1 orange
½ cup ketchup	1 Tbsp Dijon mustard	1 tsp salt
1 tsp black pepper		

For the sauce, heat the oil and add onions, cook until soft. Add the rest of the ingredients and cook on medium heat until reduced to half.

Cool and remove the cinnamon sticks.

Instructions

Grill the quail on medium-high heat for 3 minutes. Flip and brush with the sauce. Cover and cook for 4 minutes and flip and brush with sauce, cook for 1 minute, and remove from the grill.

You can serve with the remaining sauce.

God's Grilling Technique:

Ingredients:

A Teachable Spirit	1 Cup Humility
1 Cup Servanthood	2 Cups Patience

Instructions:

Mix the teachable spirit with Servanthood. Slow cook with Patience. Turning periodically, add Humility and continue turning until you become an example of a Mentor, with the values of the Kingdom of God.

KNOWLEDGE

Gourmetian informs us that a Great chef must have "An encyclopedic knowledge of food and ingredients. It is important to know the seasonality of the ingredients and the methods of cooking.

It's in reading this that I realized that in restaurants, you sometimes see a dish on various menus and in brackets (Seasonal). Chefs, my humble apologies. I have visited restaurants, and sometimes the waiters say that they are out of items, and I normally remark, or, to my defense, mutter, well then close your doors.

I sincerely apologize for my ignorance.

Just as I had to learn that God works in times and seasons. We never know how long the season will last. Each season God has us in can be seasons of rest, wilderness, peace, and learning.

We must be able to recognize the season and grow in each season. I believe that the quicker we learn and move in obedience, the shorter the season.

Some say that knowledge is power, and some say that knowledge can destroy. I want this book to be uplifting and a book of enlightenment. I prefer to write that knowledge is power only when used in the right way. Understanding the knowledge given and the wisdom to know how to apply the knowledge is what gives us success.

Let us see how *Oxford* defines knowledge. Knowledge is facts, information, and skills acquired by a person through experience and education.

In a school environment, learning can be both practical and theoretical.

Let us see how God views knowledge.

Christianity.com says that knowledge refers to examples, truths, and commands that God wants us to follow.

It's my understanding that knowledge in the Bible is just that – understanding.

With God, knowledge is all about understanding the knowledge with wisdom and revelation.

He gives so many scriptures on knowledge.

The Bible tells us that we should have Wisdom, Knowledge, and Understanding. Knowledge is based on facts; Understanding is the ability to glean the meaning of these facts, and Wisdom is in the knowing of how to proceed or what to do based on these facts. **Daniel 1:17**

Proverbs 2:6 says the Lord gives wisdom; from his mouth comes knowledge and understanding.

Proverbs 1:7 says that the fear of the Lord is the beginning of knowledge, but fools despise wisdom and instruction.

Psalm 119:66 tells us – Teach me knowledge and good judgment.

Recipe for Lemon Roasted Asparagus:

Ingredients:
1 lg bunch of asparagus
1-2 cloves minced garlic
¼ tsp salt
1 tbsp lemon zest
Parmesan cheese (Optional)

1 tbsp olive oil
1 small finely chopped shallot
¼ tsp black pepper
1 tbsp lemon juice

Instructions:
Preheat oven 400°F
Cut off the ends of the asparagus.
Toss the asparagus with olive oil, salt, pepper, garlic, shallot, and lemon zest. Place them out in a single layer on a baking sheet.
Roast until tender, 15 minutes. They must be tender yet still have a vibrant color.
Place on a dish and finish with a sprinkling of a few drops of lemon juice, some zest, and cheese.

God's Recipe for Roasted Asparagus:

Ingredients:
1 Cups of Understanding
1 ½ Cups Revelation
1 Cup of Knowledge

3 Cups of Wisdom
1 Cup Anointing Oil

Instructions:
Toss Understanding, Knowledge, and Revelation with oil.
Roast until tenderhearted and filled with Wisdom.
To test if it's good, knock with sound judgment.

POSITION

Your position is not about power but one of responsibility.

Always remember that what goes wrong is your responsibility. As a chef, even if it was someone else's mistake. A strong person takes ownership of the mistakes made under their leadership. This is not only in leadership. A person of character admits to their mistakes or errors.

The definition of position, as per *Oxford,* means to put or arrange (someone or something) in a particular way.

Collins Dictionary used it as a countable noun and gives the meaning as Position in a company or organization. This is the meaning we are using in the context of what is being written.

As it pertains to the cooking world and environment, there are various positions.

Each has a responsibility in the kitchen. The sous chef does little cooking; he manages the kitchen and staff.

The chef has the position or responsibility of setting the tone in the kitchen. Selecting the right staff and training them is also his responsibility. So, when anything goes wrong, it is also his responsibility.

In researching the various positions, I was amazed at the various positions that are needed, as they are all specialized in the kitchen. Some examples of various positions in the culinary world are the Sauce Chef, Meat Chef, Pastry Chef, Butcher Chef, and these are just to name a few.

What does position mean spiritually or how does it pertain biblically?

Some popular verses we hear are Position yourself to be used by God. God is positioning you. Position yourself for battle, to name a few.

When position is not always about power but responsibility, what goes wrong in our lives, we take responsibility, but what goes right is God.

We must be mindful that we must always position ourselves where God wants us. That is our responsibility. Staying in the position God has for us will guarantee living a victorious life.

When we position ourselves with God, it carries certain responsibilities.

Matthew 22:36-40: Love God before self and others

Mark 16:15: Preach the gospel to everyone.

Galatians 6:1-3: Help others when they fall to get back on the right track.

Titus 3:1-7: Do what is good because of the Grace of God.

These are just a few that come to mind. It's what we learn early in our Christian Walk.

Sometimes in our personal lives, especially through trials that our current position is not our final destination.

Recipe for Unleavened Bread
Ingredients:

2 cups all-purpose flour
1 ½ cups warm water
2 tbs olive oil

2 cups whole wheat flour
2 tsp salt

Instructions:
Combine all the dry ingredients.
Add olive oil and then slowly add the water while kneading. Using the dough hook, knead for 8 minutes. Take the dough out and knead by hand for another 3 minutes until smooth.
Cover the dough and place it in a warm area for 30 minutes.
Divide the dough into 4 pieces and brush with olive oil. Let it rest for 30 minutes.
Heat the oven to 500°F.
Flatten the dough and place it on a baking sheet sprinkled with cornmeal. Bake for 4 minutes, poking any air bubbles with a fork.

Serve immediately or place it into a plastic bag when cooled to prevent it from getting hard. Leftovers stay fresh for 2 days at room temperature or 3 months when they are frozen.

God's Recipe for Unleavened Bread:

1 Cup Anointing Oil
1 Cup Prayer

4 Cups of Faith
2 Cups Praise

Combine Faith, Anointing Oil, Prayer, and Praise.
Cooking Time: Position yourself in Worship until breakthrough and victory.

Note by Wikipedia: Bread making in biblical times was difficult and time-consuming. The grain had to be milled, and it was left for the women to do. Each home stored its own grain, and it is estimated that it required at least three hours of daily effort to produce enough flour to make sufficient bread for a family of five.

AIMED AT COOKING YOUR BEST AT ALL TIMES

There is no great chef anywhere who does not seek to be the best at providing the best food. From using the finest and best ingredients to keeping abreast of the latest techniques.

Being the best takes hard work, passion, dedication, humility, commitment, and having very high expectations.

You must be on top of the game, seeking to continuously develop your skills.

Sometimes, there may be limitations, but this is where you rely on ability and creativity to be able to attain the highest quality dish that pleases the customer.

Some chefs and restaurants sacrifice quality for quantity. There are no shortcuts in the food business. You either serve the best or you risk giving your food and restaurant a less-than-desirable reputation.

Biblically, our aim should be to become the man or woman that God has called us to be.

Our aim is to fulfill His plan and purpose for our lives.

Just as a chef must cook food that is pleasing to the customers, so too we must be passionate about God. He calls us to love Him with all our hearts, and with all our souls, with our mind, and with all our strength. **Mark 12:30-31**

Pleasing God and aiming to be the best in His Kingdom requires humility, a heart of servitude, and we need to be loving, kind, and forgiving.

We must always be thankful, having an attitude of gratitude.

We must develop our gifts of the Holy Spirit, and our lives must also show the fruits of the Spirit, which are Love, Joy, Peace, Patience, Kindness, Faithfulness, Generosity, Gentleness, and Self-control.

Our lives must please God, and others must see the God in us.

Our mission is to hear Him say at the end – **Matthew 25:21** "Well done, good and faithful servant."

No matter what we do in life, we should always strive to be the best. God promises to prosper the work of our hands. **Deuteronomy 30:9**.

Commit all our ways to the Lord, trust in Him and He will do it. **Psalm 37:5.**

Scripture Recipe

This is a surprise recipe.
I thought it would be a fun idea for you to go to the scriptures to find the ingredients.

Preheat oven to 350 degrees

Ingredients:

2 ½ Cups Leviticus 2:2   ¾ Tsp Galatians 5:9
¼ Tsp Matthew 5:13   1 Tbsp Proverbs 7:17
¼ Cup 1 Chronicles 12:40   ½ Tsp Matthew 13:33

Combine the above in a bowl.

½ Cup Psalm 55:21   1 Cup Psalm 119:103
2 Isaiah 10:14

Instructions:

In another bowl, combine Psalm 55:21 and Psalm 119:103. Beat for 1 min.
Add Isaiah 10:14 beat for a further 1 min.
Slowly add the ingredients of the first bowl to the 2nd bowl. Mix at a slow speed and combine.
When it is mixed properly, turn off the blender.

Take the baking sheet, place the parchment paper. Drop a spoonful of the mixture on the sheet.

Bake for 12-14 minutes.

I sincerely hope that this recipe turned out great.

Prayer

Heavenly Father, we thank you for blessing us, for protecting us, and for all that concerns us. Thank you for providing for us daily. Just as you have promised to give us daily manna, whether it is spiritual manna, physical manna, or emotional manna.

Your mercies are new every day, so we thank you for your merciful hand that is on us and our families.
Thank you for being our Shepherd, and that we shall not want.

Bless our hands and prosper the work of our hands and all that we undertake to do.
Bless our kneading bowls and baskets, and may we always have more than enough, so that we can give.
Replenish everything that we give out.

We pray this in Jesus' mighty name,

Amen.

BIBLE BREAD

My Bible is my go-to source for everything.
When you make the bible a part of your daily life, God's word will certainly change you.
You will become so close to Him that you will have that relationship that builds you, and also build your faith.
You become so spiritually strong that nothing will shake your faith as you build your trust in the Lord.

In researching the Bible to see the various kinds of foods that were part of the daily diet in both the Old and New Testaments, I saw the following foods that were eaten.
Figs; Lentils; Nuts, Apricots, Bread (Unleavened), Lamb, Stews, Leeks, Melons, Olives, Pomegranates, Duck, Quail, and Barley.
I tried to use recipes that included those foods.

Each chapter in the Bible is like a slice of Bread.
Every verse, consider it a snack.
Let prayer be the Butter and sweet praise be the Jelly.

We will never have to eat dry bread.

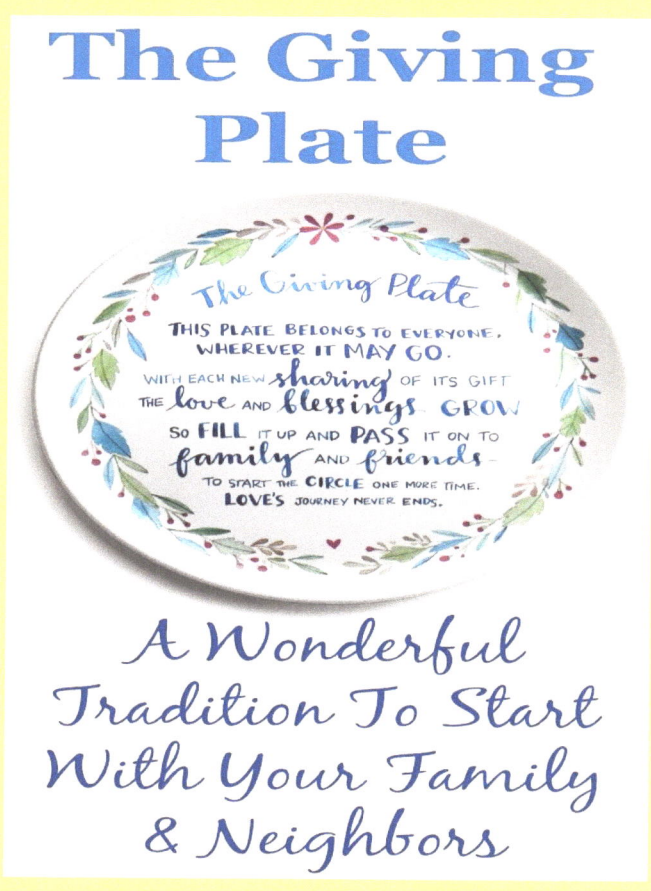

The Giving Plate was inspired by Gary and Debra Kelso in April 2020. It is a tradition between Family and Friends that encourages people to Pay it Forward by passing along a plate filled with food.

Notes:

- All Scriptures came from the NKJ
- Webster's, Collins & Oxford Dictionaries were used.
- Bible Hub, Bible Gateway, and the Bible were used for research.
- Qualities and what makes a great chef came from merging Forketers, Gourmetian, and Restaurant Blog.
- All recipes came from Food Network, All Recipes, Living By Design, and Recipetineats.

Appendix

Cooking with God was such a joyful book to write. As an amateur cook, I strive to cook foods that my family can enjoy.
I often try new recipes, and yes, I do add my own ingredients and amend some recipes to give them my signature.
I honestly believe that God has a great sense of humor.

Always remember, to become a great Chef, it requires Commitment, Passion, and Hard Work, among the important qualities. You need to develop these skills daily to be the best. You must be dedicated to your craft.

As a child of God, we must also be dedicated to God. How do we do this?
By committing our lives to Him, having that Passion for Him, and reading His word daily. Staying in His presence and worshipping Him.
Always seeking Him, not always asking but honoring Him, worshipping Him for WHO He is.
In all our ways acknowledge Him and He will direct our paths (**Proverbs 3:6**)

Isaiah 61:1 – Be dedicated as He commanded us….

Deuteronomy 28:5 – Blessed shall be your baskets and your kneading bowls.

I could never put pen to paper unless inspired by the Holy Spirit. This book is all God.

May God bless you and your family.
Walk into His blessings with Love.

Loving Jesus satisfies my very soul. He is my everything!

From my heart to yours,

Kathy

www.ingramcontent.com/pod-product-compliance
Lightning Source LLC
Chambersburg PA
CBHW041431120626
46547CB00002B/168